THE ROAD *to* NOW

Kesha Powell

ISBN 979-8-89130-844-2 (paperback)
ISBN 979-8-89130-845-9 (digital)

Christian Faith Publishing
832 Park Avenue
Meadville, PA 16335
www.christianfaithpublishing.com

Printed in the United States of America

This book would not be possible without the love, care, and guidance of Jesus Christ, who is my everything and who kept me during the negligent paths I took.

To my husband, Remus, who is also my friend, mentor, business partner, and so much more than I feel I deserve. Oh, how God blessed me with you, my love!

To my kids, Joshua, Jasmine, and Harold, and my grandkids, Christopher and Tinsley, may you find the path to your true identity in Christ, live it to the fullest, and bring glory and honor to YHWH (he who exists), the lover of your soul, and let no one steal it from you. I love you all!

Contents

ACKNOWLEDGMENTS

To Mama (Priscilla Bennett 1934–2022), thank you for introducing me to God, bringing me to church, and saying a prayer that brought Remus into my life. I am forever grateful.

To my siblings, Bro. Jesse and Sis. Cathy Duplantis, and the Covenant Church family.

To my girl, D (Doral), who was the first protector I had in elementary school.

Also, to Jennifer, for the word to finish this book.

To Colin and Shantel (life-long bond), Kim (K-Bizzle) P., Diane (my HuneyDizzle), Phyllis F., Laura C., Nelann (my Lannie), Kim B., Ella R., Wendy J., Antionette M., and all of Skandy's sweet customers who believed in me by buying my skin-care products.

To my precious spiritual mamas, Alice, Marlene, Margaret, Ethel, Betty, Nettie, and a host of so many others that I learned from to utilize the knowledge I gained from being in their company. A special thanks to the staff at Christian Faith Publishing for taking on this project. May Adonai richly bless everyone there.

FOREWORD

After reading this book and asking my thoughts on it, I was honored as Kesha's friend and spiritual sister and as a licensed counselor. I was deeply aware of what it took from her to relive her past, but through obeying God's prompting, she has birthed a ministry that can bring healing to the lost and broken. I believe one of the most powerful tools for healing is someone who has walked in your shoes and not only survived but thrived. As a substance abuse counselor who, myself, overcame addiction, I had clients who would say, "Do you know what I'm going through? How did you do it?" Kesha tells it like it is—her complete rock honesty, the trauma she endured, and the choices she made took her down a path. That was almost one of no return, but Kesha doesn't leave the reader there. Ultimately, this is a book of hope, healing, and restoration. It's about a god of love, Marcy, and his amazing grace. I got someone who performs miraculous healings every day. I've experienced it, Kesha experienced it, and so can you!

—Phyllis Resmondo, Field MSCA

CHAPTER 1

Life's Many Roads

I want to begin my story by defining what the word "road" means. (1) A road is a long piece of hard ground that is built between two places so that people can drive or ride easily from one place to the other. (2) A road is a wide way leading from one place to another, especially with a specially prepared surface which vehicles or pedestrians can use. Also there are many types of roads, such as earthen, gravel, murrum, kankar, WBM, bituminous, and concrete.

Every human being on this planet has, at one point or another, had to make use of a road to get to their destination. In fact, you can't get anywhere without traveling on a road; however, all roads are not the same. For those of us who are the much traveled have encountered many different types of roads, a series of events or a course of action that will lead to a particular outcome or a particular course or direction taken or followed. "Enter through the narrow gate. For wide is the gate and broad is the road that leads to destruction, and many enter through it. But small is the gate and narrow the road that leads to life, and only a few find it" (Mt 7:13–14 NIV).

It's my prayer that as you read this book, it will help you to identify the current road you're on and decide whether or not it's purposeful or destructive, plus give you the tools to gather up the courage to make and take an exit toward your destiny. This book is my story of the accounts or shall I call them roads that has brought me to my life that is now.

I'm going to take you through the struggles of a girl trying to find her purpose and learn who she really is in every road she travels.

Are you going to come along as I travel the road to now?

CHAPTER 2

Abused Road
Identity Theft

Now, let's look at how the word "abuse" is defined. Abuse is the improper usage or treatment of an entity, often to, unfairly or improperly, gain benefit. Abuse can come in many forms, such as physical or verbal maltreatment, injury, assault, violation, rape, unjust practices, crimes, or other types of aggression. To these descriptions, one can also add the Kantian notion of the wrongness of using another human being as means to an end rather than as ends in themselves. Some sources describe abuse as "socially constructed," which means there may be more or less recognition of the suffering of a victim at different times and societies (Wikipedia).

In a recent US study, the prevalence of child sexual abuse is difficult to determine because it is often not reported; experts agree that the incidence is far greater than what is reported to authorities. CSA is also not uniformly defined, so statistics may vary. Statistics below represent some of the research done on child sexual abuse.

The US Department of Health and Human Services' Children's Bureau report on child maltreatment for 2010 found that 9.2 percent of victimized children were sexually assaulted. US studies by David Finkelhor, director of the Crimes against Children Research Center, show that 1 in 5 girls and 1 in 20 boys is a victim of child sexual abuse. Self-report studies show that 20 percent of adult females and 5–10 percent of adult males recall a childhood sexual assault or sexual abuse incident. During a one-year period in the US, 16 percent of youth ages 14 to 17 had been sexually victimized. Over the course of their lifetime, 28 percent of US youth ages 14 to 17 had been sexually victimized. Children are most vulnerable to CSA between the ages of 7 and 13.

According to a 2003 National Institute of Justice report, 3 out of 4 adolescents who have been sexually assaulted were victimized by someone they knew well. A Bureau of Justice Statistics report shows 1.6 percent (sixteen out of one thousand) of children between the ages of 12 and 17 were victims of rape/sexual assault.

A study conducted in 1986 found that 63 percent of women who had suffered sexual abuse by a family member also reported a rape or attempted rape after the age of 14. Recent studies have all concluded similar results.

Children who had an experience of rape or attempted rape in their adolescent years were 13.7 times more likely to experience rape or attempted rape in their first year of college. A child who is the victim of prolonged sexual abuse usually develops low self-esteem, a feeling of worthlessness, and an abnormal or distorted view of sex. The child may become withdrawn and mistrustful of adults and can become suicidal.

Children who do not live with both parents as well as children living in homes marked by parental discord, divorce, or domestic violence have a higher risk of being sexually abused.

Child sexual abuse is not solely restricted to physical contact; such abuse could include noncontact abuse, such as exposure, voyeurism, and child pornography.

Compared to those with no history of sexual abuse, young males who were sexually abused were five times more likely to cause teen pregnancy, three times more likely to have multiple sexual partners, and two times more likely to have unprotected sex, according to the study published online and in the June print issue of the *Journal of Adolescent Health*. (National Center for Victims of Crime internet is cited for this article.)

Wow! That is so sad but terribly true. That's why I'm writing the story because I want that number to change! For me one that falls victims to sexual abuse is one too many. It pains me to begin my story with this alarming truth.

I was five years old, and still I can remember this road like I had traveled it yesterday. Although God has healed me, I'm still removing the deep wounds from having this road forced on me. Surely, if I had a choice in the matter, this is one path that I would never have taken voluntarily especially at such a young age. As you read in the article, most people are abused not by strangers but by someone familiar to them. With that being said, I begin my story. I was five years old, and yet I can still recall that day which changed my life. I'm tearing up as I'm writing these words, and though God has since healed me from that horrific abuse that no child should ever endure, just to relive it as I share it with you still pains me because 'til this day, the molester still denies his participation in that act. I guess he believes that by denying it, it never happened. Strangely, I wasn't the only one he molested; I was just the youngest, and this is where I begin my account of that day.

My mother had gone to work, and the abuser was supposed to be babysitting me; however, that wasn't what he had on his agenda.

That morning was different from any other. I can't explain how except that it seemed like an audience in the realm of the spirit was attentively looking as this horrifying event took place. I remember that morning was very still and the house was filled with an arctic blast full of evil lurking to attack its victims. I made the plural statement because both parties involved are victims. Evil cannot manipulate and manifest unless there is a human it can live in.

"Stay alert! Watch out for your great enemy, the devil. He prowls around like a roaring lion, looking for someone to devour" (1 Pt 5:8 NLT).

Also, read Mark 5:1–13 to get a better understanding of demon possession.

At that age, you're not familiar with the reality of that very thing because there's still so much innocence and virtue of being a child. It's even worse when your innocence is abducted and held hostage by someone you should have been able to trust with those very sacred things at that childhood age.

I remember being given a box of cereal to eat as he had me on top of the kitchen table forcing his penis inside of me, and I started crying and screaming, saying, "Stop! It's hurting me. Please stop!" He said, "Shut up! Or I'mma whip you with this belt!"

It was at that point the earth stood still, and I felt like I went into this sort of cocoon in which at that age I got wrapped up inside of the metaphysical thing or whatever you want to call it. I felt like something came over me.

After that, all I know is that I was different. I can't explain it, but I didn't feel like myself. I know you're thinking "But you're only five years old." Believe me, when you experience abuse of this type and nature, you know. The war inside your head begins! So many thoughts, so many questions are bombarding you; it's like an explosion went off with your emotions. At that point, an open door of a sexual perversion spirit attaches itself to you and makes you think that you were born that way.

"So God created human beings in his own image. In the image of God he created them; male and female he created them" (Gn 1:27 NLT).

"For we are not fighting against flesh-and-blood enemies, but against evil rulers and authorities of the unseen world, against mighty powers in this dark world, and against evil spirits in the heavenly places" (Eph 6:12 NLT).

As a child, how do you deal with all that at the moment? You become "weird"! The feeling of guilt, shame, disgust, and even self-hatred. People are not just born that way. Now all the expressions come out differently than others. For one, it could be prostitution, thinking her/his body isn't worthy of love and relations in the godly setting or his standard for man and woman. Also there's gender confusion. I used to want to be a boy so bad that at times I would face the toilet and pee standing up. For another, it could be self-mutilation. Then there's not wanting to feel any emotion and you self-destruct by way of drinking alcohol and drug use to go into a state of numbness because you're too afraid of killing yourself, and besides, don't you go to hell for that? Right? At least, that's what I believe. I now realize all of the above can send you there just as quick too! I'm laughing and POL (praising out loud) for the Lord kept me!

It's amazing how when you go through something traumatic, you force your brain to try to forget it, and some things you do, but some things are so deeply embedded you can never forget them. I now have come to realize that hurt people hurt people. Although it's no excuse. How else can you explain someone hurting someone with no sense of consciousness while they're performing that sexual act on you whether you're a child or an adult? However, my story continues. Like I said, I was five years old when I remember the first abuse of that sexual sort, and as I began to grow older, I realized that the person/abuser was suddenly gone for a very long time. Yes, this was a relative. However, it wasn't just me but my three brothers also were being sexually abused. I don't know how long it went on for them, but for me, all I recall is that one incident; maybe it happened more than once, but I somehow have blocked that out of my mind.

Being the youngest out of ten children and not coming from a wealthy family, your parents had to work, and I believe that's how a lot of kids get caught in that vicious sexual abuse cycle. Parents are working trying to make a living and needing someone who they think they can trust to care for their children, but that's how most of them get abused, and it's never talked about because we don't talk about such things and shame the family, right? It all gets tucked underneath the rug, and nothing never happens, so the victims feel like no one cares to fight for them, and I believe if more victims spoke out immediately when something like this happens, things would be different and people's lives would be totally transformed and how they see themselves because they had someone that cared enough to fight for them to help keep them safe.

I'm speaking out now because it's time. I've met too many young girls and boys who have experienced the same thing happen to them, and I want to encourage those who are reading this book if it has happened to you, please say something, or if you know about someone, find ways to help them because they're hurting on the inside and they don't know how to deal with it.

CHAPTER 3

Adolescent Road In My Feelings

Growing up, I spent a lot of time alone because my mom worked a lot and my other siblings who were much older than me had their own families and homes, and the siblings that did live at home worked jobs. So every once in a while, we would have relatives come over. I had nieces who were the same age as me. I know that's pretty odd, but my mom and two of her daughters were pregnant at the same time, which afforded me the opportunity to have playmates, or shall I say prey-mates? Remember, hurt people hurt other people. We would always play this game call "house" in which someone had to be the mom and someone had to be the dad, and I learned this from playing with my neighbor. She would be the dad and I would be the mom, and she performed and showed me things that little kids shouldn't do, but I believe she was sexually abused also for her to show me the things that she showed me.

So when my nieces would come over to visit, I would get them to play this "game" also. As I look back, it's interesting how the sexual abuse was considered a game, and I believe it's done that way to get the child to go along with it because children by nature are trusting toward adults or those that appear older than them, so quite naturally, they're gonna believe them, and that's how it starts by getting into the mind to make them believe what they're doing is not wrong. It's more than wrong; it's satanic and pure evil to steal a child's innocence away before they could understand what has been done to them.

After the molester had went away, things for me were not normal coming up as a child. Like I said before, I didn't want to be a girl because I thought being a girl made me weak and that if I were a boy, this would never happen to me again. Oh, how that is so far from the truth. I was too afraid to tell anyone how I felt because in those days, you just kept quiet about a lot of things that happened in the family, and you didn't talk about it. When you were around the person who sexually assaulted you, you just act like nothing ever happened. Actually, I believe that being around the person who sexually abused you doubles the torment. I think growing up, I was more afraid of my parents not believing me, even though they did believe me when I shared my experience some twenty years later. I know my life would have been different if I was able to go to them and tell them what happened to me and to get counseling to help with the mental trauma that accompanies the physical and sexual abuse.

I'm so thankful to God that I had a sister who was ten years older than me and became very protective of me. Maybe she felt something had happened by the way I was acting. Nevertheless, she took me under her wing like I was her own child while my mom worked, and that made all the difference in the world. Although it didn't change what happened to me, it did help with the process of me becoming the person I am now. However, growing up and having her there made it a little bit more easy for me until she had gotten married too and moved out of the house, which devastated me. Yes, I did have other sisters, but she was the closest to my age even though we were ten years apart. My other sisters had their own families, so I had become angry, rebellious, and just didn't care about anything anymore. It truly makes a difference having someone you can truly trust and be honest with about things that you're going through (without judgment) and what you're experiencing, and it really helps if that person is a believer in Jesus Christ and can share godly wisdom and pray you through what you're going through like she did for me.

I didn't tell her what I went through until I became a grown woman, and she told me she had a feeling I did because of what happened to our three brothers. She wasn't too surprised at the sexual trauma I suffered, but she was so glad I told her instead of keeping it to myself because she now had children of her own. Remember, I mentioned earlier that the person who abused me had went away, and it allowed me and my brothers to grow up with some normalcy after that, but it changed all of us to the degree of them being gay and me thinking I was but wasn't sure what that meant.

During my adolescent to teenage years, I was very rebellious and wild doing what I wanted to do, and my mom constantly threatened to send me away to some sort of group home. If I only could have told her why I was like I was, but I couldn't because I felt I really couldn't talk to her and she didn't make it easy to. I was the last of ten children, so quite naturally, she probably had some issues she dealt with on her own, being preoccupied with taking care of the family because my dad wasn't in his rightful place as a husband and a father. But the heavy drinking just made the issues worse between my mom and dad. The chaos between them at times seemed like I was in a movie, and I would wonder when will the movie be over so I can go back to a regular life, whatever that meant. Sometimes, I felt sorry for my mom because she was the one who had to deal with my dad passing out with his pants soaked from urinating on himself and empty pockets for having spent his paycheck and nothing left to help with the household needs. Nevertheless, in spite of all that, she was able to keep things together, and I truly admire her for that looking back now as I am an adult with my own family and understanding the needs of the household budget. We were poor; no, let me rephrase that, we were po! I didn't even know it because she worked really hard at trying to make sure we had what we needed, and she was very gifted in sewing, cooking, music, and writing. We went to church every Sunday and spent Saturdays getting ready because her dad was a preacher and going to church was the eleventh commandment in our family.

It's interesting to me how we never missed Sunday school and church service, but there was so much dysfunction that went on in our home. Nevertheless, she did what she knew by bringing us to church so we could learn about God and the wonderful gift of salvation that his Son Jesus Christ offers us when he died on the cross and was raised to life again three days later. I remember my first perspective of God began when I was eight years old going to my first Sunday school class. I thought, if he was as good as people said, then why did this bad stuff happen to me? Where was he? So at the age of twelve, I made the conscious decision to give my life to Christ and to make him my Lord and Savior. Then as I was getting back on track to being normal, I guess, the unthinkable happens at a place that I was starting to feel comfortable, church.

It was a Saturday evening after a choir rehearsal, and one of the young men there who was so active and admired by all the young churchgoing girls was walking me home, and little did I know he was a predator. He tricked me into walking a little farther with him, and I was a young naive girl and trusted him because after all we went to the same church. He grabbed a bottle, broke it, put it up to my neck, made me keep still while he pulled my pants down, and raped me, and I was crying and screaming, saying, "Stop!" He told me I better shut up or he was gonna stick that bottle in my neck and kill me, and I'm thinking to myself, *How could this be happening again?*

I managed to break loose and started running. There was a puddle of water there, and I stepped in, and my clothes got full of mud. I didn't care. I ran as fast as I could as he chased me, and eventually, I made it home because we didn't live that far from the church. As I made it inside, my sister was there, and she asked me what happened, and I was too afraid and too ashamed to tell her, but nevertheless, I trusted her and I told her what happened, and she was angry. She went to my mom and told her what happened also, and then she went to the pastor, but interestingly though, the police was never called because like I said, when things happen like that and because it was the church, nothing was done. It was just tucked under the rug, and they were going to have a good talk with him so he wouldn't do that to anyone else. Do you see how the cycle continues?

Then I remember telling my sister that I didn't like boys and I didn't want to be a girl. The door that was shut when I received Christ is now kicked wide open again! Then she took me by the hand and prayed for me and showed me these verses of scripture in the Bible: "If a man sleeps with a man as with a woman, they have both committed a detestable act" (Lv 20:13 CSB). "Don't you know that the unrighteous will not inherit God's kingdom? Do not be deceived: No sexually immoral people, idolaters, adulterers, or males who have sex with males, 10 no thieves, greedy people, drunkards, verbally abusive people, or swindlers will inherit God's kingdom" (1 Cor 6:9–11 CSB).

Then she lovingly explained what those scriptures meant and how they applied to me. You see, God is the creator of man, and then he created woman. He is not confused about what he chose to make each of us because he also has an amazing purpose for each one of us should we choose to follow his plan and path.

"You made all the delicate, inner parts of my body and knit me together in my mother's womb. Thank you for making me so wonderfully complex! Your workmanship is marvelous—how well I know it" (Ps 139:13–14 NLT).

These verses of scripture undeniably say that before each of us were born, God knew us, and he knew exactly what we would be, a boy or a girl. There's no in between; there's no deciding after you're born. God is the creator of all that exist, and the creator is always greater than the creation, and he also knew the best way for the operation of his creation.

Let me help you further understand what I meant by this. I created a lotion after going through kidney cancer and multiple surgeries. I had the directions on the back of the label on how the lotion is to be used in order to get the desired results from it. I also had a disclaimer on how it is not to be used. It also stated what could happen if it's used the wrong way. Now let's apply that to the scripture we just read.

God said he knew exactly what he made each of us, and in order for us to live our best life, which would give him glory by doing that, we will have to follow the simple instructions he stated in the Bible. This is really easy, but Satan did his best to try to make God looked like a liar, and we knew he's the real liar. He's the one that wanted a lot of company in hell, and by the way, hell was never created for us; it was created for him and all the fallen angels that he tricked into going along with his scheme against God Almighty.

"One day the members of the heavenly court came to present themselves before the Lord, and the accuser, Satan, came with them. 'Where have you come from?' the Lord asked Satan. Satan answered the Lord, 'I have been patrolling the earth, watching everything that's going on'" (Jb 1:6–7 NLT).

"The thief's purpose is to steal and kill and destroy. My purpose is to give them a rich and satisfying life" (Jn 10:10 NLT).

"The seventy returned with joy, saying, 'Lord, even the demons are subject to us in your name!' And he said to them, 'I saw Satan fall like lightning from heaven. Behold, I have given you authority to tread upon serpents and scorpions, and over all the power of the enemy; and nothing shall hurt you. Nevertheless do not rejoice in this, that the spirits are subject to you; but rejoice that your names are written in heaven'" (Lk 10:17–20 RSV).

I was comforted for a while until I met a girl at church who was very promiscuous and befriended me. She began telling me about all her sexual escapades with guys, and she had a way of putting it in such a way that it seemed so exciting and alluring, and so I took the bait hook, line and sinker. She made it seem like I was missing out on something if I wasn't doing what she was doing. There's an old cliché that says "Show me your company and I'll tell you who you are," and oh, boy, I so became like the company I kept because what you tolerate will contaminate you if you don't get away from it soon enough.

As a young child, I remembered seeing an angel and a demon fighting outside my window, and I never understood why until several years ago. Do you know there's a fight over you because you are so valuable to God and Satan will stop at nothing to try to take what God deems extremely precious, rare, and valuable? Yes! I'm referring to you! The fact that I am writing this book and you're reading it shows he was there all along, but he created us like him with a will to choose good or evil. When people do bad things, he always encourages them to do the right thing, but it's up to us to choose to do the right thing or the bad thing. However, consequences follow both choices.

Fast-forward. The year was 1990, and I'm a sixteen-year-old teenager who had been molested by a family member and raped by someone in the church, a place that should have been safe because after all, God's presence was there, right? Plus, I had two failed suicide attempts and so many sex partners; it's a miracle that I didn't contract a bunch of sexually transmitted diseases. And now I'm pregnant!

CHAPTER 4

Motherhood Road
Having Kids

I had no idea on the road that I had just taken and currently about to travel on in becoming a mother. The only thing I knew about it was I was supposed to be married first and then the children were supposed to come after because that's how God designed it to be.

"And the rib, which the Lord God had taken from man, made he a woman, and brought her unto the man. And Adam said, 'This is now bone of my bones, and flesh of my flesh: she shall be called Woman, because she was taken out of Man.' Therefore shall a man leave his mother and father and cleave unto his wife: and they shall be one flesh" (Gn 2:22–24 KJV).

Well, I quickly learned that things don't always turn out as planned, and I felt like I was in a bigger mess than ever, not realizing that God could use everything for his purpose.

"And we know that all things work together for good to them that love God, to them who are the called according to [his] purpose" (Rom 8:28 KJV).

Although to me it seemed like I had failed him miserably, I did start to love God, but I didn't fully understand him because when I was young going to church, it was a lot of religion, and religion made it hard to understand God when he created us for fellowship with him, not religion with him. So I did everything I could think of to get rid of me and the baby without it being painful because I was already in so much pain on the inside. At this point, I didn't care where I went; I just didn't want to be on earth anymore. I'm not going to go into details because it's not necessary. As you can see, I'm still here because God had a plan for me, and guess what, he definitely has one for *you*!

"'For I know the plans I have for you,' says the Lord. 'They are plans for good and not for disaster, to give you a future and a hope. In those days when you pray, I will listen. If you look for me wholeheartedly, you will find me'" (Jer 29:11–13 NLT).

After taking a whole lot of stuff I shouldn't have taken while being pregnant, thinking that it would abort the baby and kill me, none of it worked. God supernaturally intervened because he loved me so much and he knew the end from the beginning; he knew he had a great purpose for me. He knew us better than we knew ourselves, and he knew deep, deep down why I was doing it and that I really didn't wanna die. So he, in his mercy, gave me another chance to do things differently, and believe me, it was tough going through a pregnancy and not knowing what to expect because I had taken so much stuff, not knowing if my child would be normal or not. But thank God none of it had any effect, and I had a beautiful, healthy baby boy that totally changed my outlook in life because I had given birth to this little human being that now depended on me and needed me.

I think that's how it is in the rebirth process of salvation. We become these little newborn babies, and we're supposed to totally depend on God for nourishment. Jesus gives us new life by accepting his death, burial, and resurrection on the cross, and now he presents these beautiful new little babies to the Father to nurture and care for them. I like to think churches as being the nurseries for these new little babies, or that's how it should be anyway, while the word of God is being taught uncompromised, unrestricted, and helping these new lives become all that God intended them to be and to help point them and nurture them toward their purpose so they can reach their destiny on this earth.

You might ask me, was he a mistake? I will answer you undoubtably, *no*, he was not. I truly believed God wanted him here, and although I went about it the wrong way, God had a purpose and a plan for him to be born also. He was my dad's first grandson, and, oh, boy, he was totally excited about him; he bought a lot of joy to a lot of lives. I thought I was in love with his father, but how could I? I didn't really love myself and understood who I truly was, so let's just say I really, really, really, really, really liked him. We got by, but I was a young mother and irresponsible. I was stupid, dumb, and gullible. You know what? I was because I did everything I thought I could to make him love me, or shall I say really, really, really, really, really like me like I did him, but he didn't know who he was either. He spent a lot of time in and out of prison at a young age, so he didn't get a chance to experience life either, and the crowd that he hung out with was not a good one. As a matter of fact, most of them were no longer alive. He had a good mom, and she was a really nice lady, and I still liked her to this day.

However, it is the company that you keep that also sends you down the wrong road. What you tolerate will contaminate you if you don't "come to yourself" or have someone around you that can speak freely and honestly and lovingly to you. My sister would pray so much for me during that time, and although the effects of it were not seen immediately, those prayers would be answered years later. You see, God does not view time as we see time because he is eternal. Scripture says one thousand years is one day. Can you imagine praying for someone for over ten years and not see anything happen and then all of a sudden change takes place for the better?

"Dear friends, don't overlook this one fact: With the Lord one day is like a thousand years, and a thousand years like one day. The Lord does not delay his promise, as some understand delay, but is patient with you, not wanting any to perish but all to come to repentance" (2 Pt 3:8–9 CSB).

Well, that's what happened to me, only it took for me to have two more kids by two different men, which meant I now had three kids and three baby daddies! What a mess! But God specializes in messes. Just think of all the occupations Jesus Christ could've had. He had the occupation of a carpenter. What do carpenters do? I'm glad you asked. Carpenters specialize in making beautiful things out of ordinary materials. That's what Jesus does; he takes the mess that we've made of our lives, and when we surrender our whole heart to him, he turns us into something wonderful and beautiful as we are presented brand-new creations to our heavenly Father!

"Therefore, if anyone is in Christ, he is a new creation; the old has passed away, and see, the new has come! Everything is from God, who has reconciled us to himself through Christ and has given us the ministry of reconciliation. That is, in Christ, God was reconciling the world to himself, not counting their trespasses against them, and he has committed the message of reconciliation to us" (2 Cor 5:17–19 CSB).

CHAPTER 5

Love Road
Meeting My Husband

It's now 1998, and I had just given birth to my last child and still live at home with my mom, with many failed relationships, and I decided that love didn't live here anymore! So I vowed to never get married because there were no good men out there. So why bother? I realized I was looking at it all wrong. I had to rediscover me and my true identity before I was ready to become a wife material. Heck, let me be honest. I wasn't even good mom material because I was young and didn't understand a lot.

By this time, my mom had gotten older because she had me when she was forty. She always fussed a lot at me but still kept the kids because she loved them, and I knew she loved me, plus I worked, and the money helped with taking care of the house. It was a win-win for all of us. I helped out with the bills, and I had an in-house babysitter. I remembered my mom telling me that she's getting too old to watch kids and I needed a husband and that she was going to pray and ask God to send me a good man. And after laughing at her for a few minutes for making that statement, I pondered those words as they began to penetrate my thoughts about getting married.

The next day, I got news of a friend of mine who was getting married, and I thought to myself, *Are you kidding me? Now if she can get a husband, I know I can!* That's when I said an honest, heartfelt prayer to God that I soon forgot about after I prayed. However, God never forgot it!

"In my distress I called upon the Lord, and cried unto my God: he heard my voice out of his temple, and my cry came before him, [even] into his ears" (Ps 18:6 KJV).

"I cried unto him with my mouth, and he was extolled with my tongue. If I regard iniquity in my heart, the Lord will not hear [me]: [But] verily God hath heard [me]; he hath attended to the voice of my prayer. Blessed [be] God, which hath not turned away my prayer, nor his mercy from me" (Ps 66:17–20 KJV).

"Give all your worries and cares to God, for he cares about you" (1 Pt 5:7 NLT).

Now, I had prayed this prayer before many years ago, but this time, I had given it a lot of thought and faith, and I believe because I forgot about it, it really gave God the opportunity to answer it. Then a few months later, I had a dream about a man, and I never saw his face, but in the dream, I was married, and I appeared to be very happy. Interesting. I had the same dream for about two months straight. Was God sending me a message? I don't know, but it really started to get my attention to the degree that I started to change in a good way. All of a sudden, I just started thinking about the type of husband I wanted, and then I reasoned to myself, "Whatever I'm looking for in a husband, I should become that in a wife." With the help of God, I just decided to change out all the bad stuff in me that I didn't want in a husband.

Now let me tell you, this did not happen overnight. This was a process, and it's still ongoing; however, I am not the person I used to be, and thank God for that! Jesus Christ had totally transformed me that sometimes I pinched myself to see if it's me.

Then in November of 1998, I met who would be my husband of twenty years (twenty-four years total) through a coworker. I was totally against blind dates because they never worked out for me in the past, but I felt an urge to meet him. We met over the phone first and talked for two weeks before we actually met in person, and he had a really good conversation, and we talked for hours until we fell asleep on the phone talking to each other.

The next thing was for us to meet!

I remember it was November 1998 at Thanksgiving time when we first saw each other face-to-face, and let me tell you, he wasn't my "type." You see, we all have this foolish notion that our "type" could be compared to a list, probably in our heads for a time period, as in not too tall, etc. In a sense, you could have what's on the list, but without Christ on the list, it'll be incomplete.

Jesus Christ gives you a new set of eyes that sees everything on that list in a much more different way, such as a certain height. He may not be 6'2", but because he's a believer and has a personal relationship with Jesus Christ, his spirit is, and he prays for and over *you*! He may be a li'l large, but because he's a tither and seed sower, his bank accounts are times two! Plus, he doesn't mind sharing it with *you*! Same goes if he's a li'l thin and his bank accounts aren't! You may want him to possess a certain eye color, but every time you look at his, they're on *you*!

What I'm saying is when the person you meet is born again through the power of Jesus Christ and his finished work on the cross, everything you see on the inside will match on the outside. I said all that to say when he's all that, God will send him your way. My husband was not born again when I met him, and I walked away from the Lord, but it was his mercy and grace plus love for me. He loaned those eyes to me because he knew I would be completely his eventually. Now Remus also would be completely his too! Because of the prayer from me, my mom, and my sister, let me tell ya, he's absolutely everything I had on my list! To Adonai be all the glory.

"'My thoughts are nothing like your thoughts,' says the Lord. 'And my ways are far beyond anything you could imagine. For just as the heavens are higher than the earth, so my ways are higher than your ways and my thoughts higher than your thoughts'" (Is 55:8–9 NLT).

"I also tell you this: If two of you agree here on earth concerning anything you ask, my Father in heaven will do it for you" (Mt 18:19 NLT).

It's now Christmas Eve, and we had been seeing each other for a little over a month. I couldn't believe how great he had been to meet my three kids, which was something you don't find often in most men, but remember, I had a list. Then he asked me, "Are their dads in their life?"

When we first talked, I had told them that my kids did not have the same dad, and he said that didn't bother him one bit. He did not judge me, which was a big plus.

I told him, "No, they weren't."

He went on further to say, "That's okay. We don't need them because I'm here now."

Later that night, he called me and asked me what was I doing for Christmas because he wanted to see me and the kids, and I immediately said, "Nothing! I'll be over there. What time?"

I really enjoyed being with him. He was a perfect gentleman opening doors for me and making sure I'm safe at night when me and the kids leave his place. By this time, Joshua was eight, Jasmine was six, and Harold was six months old. When we got there on Christmas morning, to our surprise, there were gifts everywhere! I believed the kids had more than me, but that's okay; I enjoyed watching them open the gifts he had for them plus the ones I had for them as well. It was a great first Christmas for us, and I had never been treated so kind before; plus, the kids really liked him too, and they got along well together.

A few months went by, and we decided to move in together. Back then, I didn't realize the importance of doing things God's way first; however, it all worked out for good because God knew we would both belong to him later. Then one night, I can't tell you the exact date, when I looked at him, I realized that I was deeply in love with him not because of the things but because of who he was and how he treated me and most importantly how he treated my kids. Everything we did involve them. He never wanted to see me without them. Sounded too good to be true, right? Well, when you're absolutely definite about what you want from God, you will absolutely, definitely get it, but you can't have any doubt and you can't let time chase you.

I asked him, "Would you like me to have children for you since you don't have any of your own?"

The response he gave me caused a flow of tears to roll down my face as he said, "We already have three kids. I don't need you to have a baby for me for me to love you. I prayed and asked God for a family, and that's what he gave me."

A real man doesn't have to have biological children to take care of them. It doesn't make you a man just because you can make babies. What makes you a man is when you can take care of your kids and another man's kids who's not there for whatever reason.

As the tears flowed, I thought to myself, *Is this man for real?* I pinched him, and I pinched myself. Then

I thought, *He's too good for me*. That's what the devil wanted you to think, which will cause you to self-sabotage like most women do when they meet a really good man, or that's what men do when they meet a really good woman. These feelings of unworthiness and inadequacies. Maybe Satan will send people from your past to interfere with the happiness that God is bringing you into. But that wasn't the case for us because in the beginning, I also told him about my past; we told each other everything and laid it out all on the table. We were totally truthful and honest about everything so no one could come to either one of us from our past with drama.

Let me tell you, every last one of our vows had been thoroughly tried and tested, but because our marriage was built up on the foundation of Christ, nothing could come against it because it only made us stronger all because God had sent a beautiful lady to us that would be his catalyst for Remus and me to become completely sold out for Christ. She was our insurance lady through whom we had our life and automobile policies with, and she and her husband had a church. Every time Remus and I would go there to pay our policy premiums, she would always throw these little nuggets at us, and I remembered her having such a passion and fire for Jesus Christ, and she wasn't judgmental. We weren't married at the time, but who knew God had her on assignment to help put us on the right path.

She would always end our meeting with "My husband will marry y'all for free, but you gotta do counseling first!" She didn't even say we had to be members of their church or anything; she just saw I needed and wanted to do whatever she could to help put us on the right path for God to bless us.

We got married on March 10, 2002, at their church, and things were going really well because we decided to do marriage counseling before we got married to understand the purpose of marriage, why God created it, why it's holy unto him, and how it should be lived out in his eyes. That counseling was the best gift we could have given each other and our marriage. I highly recommend it but with someone who is filled with the spirit of God and will show you in the scripture the marriage how God sees it.

"And Adam said, 'This [is] now bone of my bones, and flesh of my flesh: she shall be called Woman, because she was taken out of Man. Therefore shall a man leave his father and his mother, and shall cleave unto his wife: and they shall be one flesh'" (Gn 2:23–24 KJV).

We spent a lot of time together with the kids doing a lot of fun things, and they got to know him really well. We even started our own business (that's for another book on how we got it started). For the first time in my life, I had someone that I could really trust and love me and treated me better than I felt I deserved. My husband is a very wise man. I learned and I'm still learning a lot from him as we both learned about each other. Me meeting him was really a God thing now that I look back at it, and I'm truly grateful to God and him for not giving up on me.

CHAPTER 6

Healing Road
My Health Path

I remembered having my first health issue back in 1999, which was my gallbladder. It was so bad that I couldn't even drink water without it coming back up. I had gotten down to skin and bones before the doctors realized it was my gallbladder. Actually, he said it should have burst on me months ago, but God kept me. Next, I was diagnosed with pulmonary sarcoidosis right after, and that journey in itself was very intense as I couldn't take two steps without needing an albuterol inhaler to help me manage the rest of my steps. Not to mention I was very swollen especially my legs; they looked like elephant legs. After undergoing many tests, my doctor said that the pulmonary sarcoidosis I had was something that sixty-year-old Caucasian men get, and he was totally astounded by me having it and that there's no known cure for it; it would eventually affect my eyesight to the point that I would lose my vision.

At this time, I had not been in close fellowship with the Lord (I was cordial with him) because of what happened to me at twelve years old, but those seeds were still planted in me. I refused to accept those diagnosis, so as you could see, I was already on a path to being totally healed because I refused to accept his report. One would say those seeds that got planted in me as a young child when I went to church to hear about God and what his Son Jesus Christ did on the cross were beginning to germinate and starting to produce. I reasoned to myself that if I came through the gallbladder situation, then I could go through this; besides, I'm not supposed to have it, right? I'm not a sixty-year-old Caucasian man.

One night, as I was dealing with the symptoms from the sarcoidosis, it was really hard to breathe, and I couldn't catch my breath, and at that moment, Remus got really scared for me; he said he felt death near, and I did also. Well, all of a sudden, as I was in the hospital for two days, I started to improve so much that I got discharged. That's when he told me he made a deal with God that if he would heal me, he would serve him for the rest of his life.

However, that was only the beginning of what I would go through health-wise.

"Who hath believed our report? And to whom is the arm of the Lord revealed?" (Is 53:1 KJV)

We didn't stay long at the church we got married in because God had a plan, and we were now at another ministry in which we were both very active. Remus and I were now headed in a totally new direction, and we were excited about it and excited about our future with God and our family.

Fast-forward to February 2004. I began experiencing some pain in my back, and I just thought maybe I picked up something too heavy or it was almost time for my friend to visit me (ladies, you know what I'm talking about). Let me just add that even with my cycle, my husband kept up with it better than me; he knew down to the date when it was time and didn't even mind getting my feminine products from the store. He once told me, "I have no issues with who I am, and besides, I don't use them."

Now it's Tuesday, and I went to my gynecologist and told her what's been going on, and she decided to do an ultrasound on me to see what's going on. She then told me she wanted me to see someone else, and I asked her if something was wrong. She paused and said, "I just wanna make sure first."

So I went to see a urologist, and he did multiple tests on me as well. Then he referred me to a specialist. Now by this time, no one had really told me anything. I'm just seeing a lot of doctors and taking a lot of tests and still in a lot of pain.

Then I got a phone call that no one wanted to get. My doctor told me she needed me to come in because she wanted to talk with me as soon as possible, and I asked her what was wrong, and she told me she could not tell me over the phone. Now my heart was really racing, and I'm very curious to the point it was hard for me to concentrate on anything.

As I sat there in the office waiting to see her, all sorts of thoughts were going through my head, and finally, my name was called, and I went into the back to talk with her. She began to tell me that I had a large mass in my left kidney that's destroying it, and she believed it was cancer and that's why I'm in so much pain. As I heard her say that, I became numb, and it felt like someone just hit me with a titanium bat. I was totally shocked and unable to speak as she asked me if I was okay. As my eyes filled up with tears, I gently told her I was fine, but on the inside, I was screaming to the top of my lungs. She told me next that we had to move quickly with this situation as it was very serious, and I told her okay. I needed some time by myself, and I would call her soon. She understood.

I began to walk like a zombie to my car all the while Remus was calling my phone to contact me about the results. At this point, I didn't want to talk to anyone, not even him. I got in the car, and I turned on worship music because I learned that from reading scriptures to my godmother, who at the time was dealing with a different form of cancer, and I would often go to her house and read the scriptures to her because she was unable to, and we really enjoyed each other's company. Plus, she said she liked the way I read to her. We would also listen to worship music. So I did what I saw her do.

It makes a difference of who you are around especially when you're going through difficult trials in your life. I must have driven for about two hours listening to anointed worship music that brought me into the very presence of the Lord, which gave me strength and hope. Once I made it home, Remus was waiting for me worried because I had not answered his call, so he figured something was wrong. It was hard for me to tell him what the doctor said because if I repeated what she said to me, that meant I accepted the diagnosis, and I definitely was not going to do that, so I just told him I had to go back and see her again, in which I did. This time, I asked the Lord to help me in asking her to show me what she saw on the test, and she did. Then as I went into prayer, which is a conversation with the Lord, I began to tell him what I saw on the test, which he knew too, and then I remembered scriptures that talked about me being healed, and I remembered how I came through the other stuff. However, this seemed way more major than the other health problems I had before; nevertheless, I believed that this would not end in death but the birth of a whole new relationship between my heavenly Father. Plus, it brought me and my husband even closer than ever.

"But he was pierced for our rebellion, crushed for our sins. He was beaten so we could be whole. He was whipped so we could be healed" (Is 53:5 NLT).

A few days later, I called my doctor and told her I'm ready to move forward with whatever she recommended, and that's when she said we needed to do surgery to remove the kidney because if we didn't, it would kill me from the poisonous toxins that got released inside my body. I then told her "Okay, let's do it," and we set the date. I told Remus my kidney had stopped working and it had to be removed, and he said, "Okay, whatever needs to be done." But we both didn't feel peace about it. I have learned that if you don't feel peace about something, it means that you are supposed to wait, which means God is saying not right now. However, if you do you have a peace about a decision, then God is giving you the green light and thumbs-up for his approval to go ahead.

It was a Tuesday afternoon when I talked to her, and she scheduled the surgery for Thursday morning at six. After we hung up, I really began to feel uneasy, and so Remus and I prayed, and I asked God that if this was okay for me to do the surgery on Thursday, then fine, but if it wasn't, I needed a undeniable sign from him stating that I should not go through with the surgery on Thursday as planned.

I want to take this opportunity to recommend that before you do anything no matter how big or small, you go to God first because he knows the end from the beginning.

"Remember the former things of old: for I [am] God, and [there is] none else; [I am] God, and [there is] none like me, declaring the end from the beginning, and from ancient times [the things] that are not [yet] done, saying, My counsel shall stand, and I will do all my pleasure" (Is 46:9–10 KJV).

It was Wednesday night, and my surgery was scheduled for six the next morning, so Remus and I had already decided to take a taxi to the hospital. We were living next door to his dad, and he agreed to get the children off to school for us. However, all that night, we still didn't have a peace about the surgery, but I didn't get a sign from God yet, and there was still time for him to approve or disapprove of this surgery in the morning.

It's now three thirty Thursday morning, and it felt different. I couldn't explain it, but suddenly, everything in the house stopped working; the lights weren't working and the phone wasn't working. Remember, I asked for an undeniable sign, and, oh, boy, was this it!

Remus asked me, "What's going on?"

I knew I paid the light bill and phone bill, and that's when the Holy Spirit reminded me of what I asked (prayed for the night before) the Lord. Immediately, I went into the living room and fell on my face before him and thanked him and worshipped him, and all of a sudden, I saw a big screen like I'm watching television, and as I continued to look, I saw the doctor come in the waiting room and tell Remus that I didn't make it, that they tried everything and then it stopped. That was a vision from the Lord, showing me what was going to happen if I went to the surgery as planned. I then asked the Lord one more time, not that I didn't believe him but I just wanted to be sure so bad.

At 9:00 AM, everything in the house started working again, and my phone rang well quite naturally. It was the doctor, and she wanted to know why I didn't show up for the surgery and what happened. I wasn't quite sure on how to explain it to her, so I just told her I chickened out. She then confessed to me that after she hung up with me that Tuesday afternoon, as she was walking to her car, the strangest feeling came over her that she never experienced before about something going wrong in the surgery and that she was trying to call me to tell me not to come for the surgery. That's when I knew I could tell her. I began to tell her that I didn't feel right about it and that the Lord told me not to go.

To my surprise, she said, "I'm glad you hearkened to his voice, and now we don't have to deal with the consequences of us not listening."

We both laughed, and then she said, "Do you want to try this again?"

I told her to give me a few days first, and she agreed. I still don't know today if she was a believer or not; however, it wouldn't surprise me if she was after having that strange encounter with me and him.

Two days passed, and she called me again and stated that it's really urgent for me to do this surgery, and I asked her what date was she looking at, and when she told me the date, I felt a relieving peace in my heart about it, so she scheduled it. My surgery was scheduled, and now it's the morning of it, and nothing in the house set off. As a matter of fact, there was such a peace in the house. I knew God had given me the green light.

So as we headed to the hospital, I went into the surgery area, and after they did my vitals, I was sent to anesthesia to get prepared for the surgery. My doctor came in to see me before they take me into surgery to ask if I had any questions or reservations about the surgery. This time also, I told her all systems were go!

Remus and I prayed with them, and then I got taken into the surgery. As the anesthesiologist told me to count backward from ten, I remembered getting to six and then I was out. The next thing I remembered was waking up to the sound of a lot of whispering voices. My eyes were still closed, and I wondered if, yes, it were angels that were talking, but it wasn't. It was a team of doctors surrounding my bed, whispering at the miraculous sight they were witnessing at the moment.

Do you want to know what they were whispering about? I'm happy to tell you they were shocked that after a seven-hour surgery that went really well and after being in recovery and now in the room, as they checked the incision, it had totally healed. They then went on to say there's no need for me to be in the hospital any longer, that I could go home, and that they had never seen anything like this ever. You know you got a supernatural miracle when the doctors declare it before you do, which is something they don't routinely do. Glory to God in the highest!

During the whole course of this ordeal, my husband was very protective of me, and he made sure that the atmosphere I was in stayed positive. If anyone came around me speaking anything less than what the word said and what we believed, he immediately removed him from me. Now that some love, isn't it? The doctors have now discharged me after going through a seven-hour surgery and the incision being healed.

The nurse that was assigned to me said, "You must know God because I have been a nurse for thirty years, and I have never seen anyone walk out of the hospital like you are after having a major organ in your body removed." And she went throughout the hospital, telling everyone what she just witnessed from taking care of me.

"The woman left her water jar beside the well and ran back to the village, telling everyone, 'Come and see a man who told me everything I ever did! Could he possibly be the Messiah?'" (Jn 4:28–29 NLT)

I believed, and, therefore, I received that I did not accept any negativity in any form from anyone, and I believe that's why I'm still here and able to share the story with you. People were going to the hospital to see me, and I was at home. How about that! I was doing good now, but eight months later, I got attacked again. Like I said earlier, there's always a fight over you. God loves you so much, and Satan hates that. By the way, the cancer that they saw in my left kidney—once they removed it and sent to the lab—came back benign, and that's what totally astounded them as my doctor told me I was the topic of every conversation. When God does something of that magnitude, it is definitely noteworthy.

It was now June 2005, and I had an acute renal failure with the right kidney, but I was beyond persuaded what God can do now as he's done so many miraculous things for me before in my body, and I reasoned to myself that this, too, will be a miraculous testimony. This time, there's a twist to it. One of my older brothers just passed away, and the family was all emotional as I was now in the hospital fighting for my life, and that fight was already fixed. It got fixed when Jesus went to the cross and rose three days later. That gave me favor for every unfavorable situation that the enemy of our souls would bring my way.

CHAPTER 7

Risen Road
Choose Life or Death

My health got worse after the funeral of my brother, and I was now tired spiritually, mentally, and physically, but I'm holding on. My husband was helping me to hold on by constantly praying for me and sitting by my side every step of the way until I got admitted into the hospital because I had stopped eating at this point, and usually, once a person stops eating, it's a sign that death is near. God used my sister to come to the house, and she forced me to go to the hospital because I wasn't going to go, and the doctor said I got there just in time. If I had stayed home another day, I would've died.

At the time, I didn't know that I was in full-blown acute renal failure, which caused me to stop urinating, which was painful also, but like I said, I was just tired, not that I didn't have any faith. I was just tired. I had to get a nephrostomy tube inserted into my back without any anesthesia because time was of the essence for me, and I could remember I saw an image that looked like

Jesus in the corner of the room as they were putting the tube in my back, which would make King Kong pass out from the pain, but the Lord was there with me, and he got me through it. Even the nurses were crying and shaking their head, saying, "How can you stand this pain?"

The tube insertion was a success, and I was now back in the room, and as I lay there in the hospital that night—it's around 2:00 AM, and it's very quiet—I began to see this tall figure with a hooded cape on him walking. I was in ICU unit, so you could see everything that pretty much went on because the doors were all open so they could keep a watch on the patients. As I saw him, I thought to myself, *I know he is not coming to get me. No, wait.* I began to pray in my heavenly language that I have received years ago, and as I was praying, he stopped in front of my room, and then he walked to the room next to me, and all of a sudden, I heard a lady screaming and crying, saying, "He's gone!" The man next to me had just died. Did I just see the death angel? Whoever, whatever it was surely came to get someone that night, and I made up my mind it was not going to be me.

The next morning, my kidney function levels were starting to stabilize, and I was now released to go home, which was a blessed event for me after what I had just witnessed the night before. However, we were now in hurricane season, and the weather was really starting to forecast a very bad hurricane headed our way.

As we watched the news, the meteorologist recommended everyone to leave town as soon as possible because this hurricane was going to be devastating, and her name was Katrina, and she was a Category 5 that took over 1,800 lives and an estimated cost of about $125 billion in damages. Our families evacuated, but we didn't because now my kidney had gotten infected and I was too weak to take the road trip, so we decided to just weather through this powerful storm, but it wasn't more powerful than our God.

In the early morning hours of August 29, 2005, we began to hear the storm then the winds. Our house began to shake as if it was in a cradle being rocked back and forth, and then the lights went out, but we were prepared. We had battery-operated radio so we could hear what was going on, and as the storm was passing, my husband and his best friend decided to go and look at the storm. As they did, that guy was peeping out of our front window, watching roofs being peeled like a banana, and the debris in the trash was blowing all around, but not for us. I stood as I watched the trash being blown through the thirteen bushes we had, but the bushes were not blowing. Truly the Lord our God was with us, protecting us from this catastrophic storm.

The next day, it was quiet, and there were debris and mess everywhere. I felt even more pain than ever. Now I was eating pain pills, but I didn't tell Remus because I didn't want to burden him anymore. He had been by dealing with the storm, taking care of the business, locking things down, and putting things away. Even in this, the Lord remained faithful as we did not lose water because he knew I needed water because that's all

I could drink at the time, and a neighbor showed up out of nowhere with a generator. As you know in Southeast Louisiana, our summers are extremely hot! The generator he provided allowed for a fan to blow air on us. We went on to stay for another week, and then we had to leave out, driving through the debris. We picked up a nail in a tire; there was no way for it to get fixed, so we drove to Baton Rouge by my oldest sister and her family. From Baton Rouge, we drove all the way to Dallas with a nail in our tire; talk about God seeing you through.

Once we got there, I now told Remus how I'm feeling and that I really needed to get to a hospital. After going to two hospitals, none of them wanted to touch me. I finally found one urologist in which he told me, "You are dying! I can't really do anything for you, but I will give you some antibiotics to help with the inflammation." And he sent me on my way.

As we were in our rented home that night, I heard God's audible voice telling me to "go home." As I told Remus, he didn't argue; he said okay. So we got a truck, packed up everything, and headed back home. God knows what is best for us, and it's always good to be quiet to hear him because he does speak audibly. He also can speak to your heart. He can also speak through other people. There's various ways that he can speak to you; don't limit him.

"So the Lord called a third time, and once more Samuel got up and went to Eli. 'Here I am. Did you call me?' Then Eli realized it was the Lord who was calling the boy. So he said to Samuel, 'Go and lie down again, and if someone calls again, say, "Speak, Lord, your servant is listening."' So Samuel went back to bed. And the Lord came and called as before, 'Samuel! Samuel!' And Samuel replied, 'Speak, your servant is listening'" (1 Sm 3:8–10 NLT).

It took us ten hours to get home, and as we were approaching the city, you could smell the stench of death everywhere. The city was so quiet, so desolate, and I remembered thinking, *Lord, you brought us back here to this?* Oh, but he was working things out for my own good. The furthest hospital was fifty miles away in a city called Houma. I had to travel there quite frequently because of my health situation, which made a lot of sense. When I got there the first time, I had to go to the ER, and as I was sitting in the ER, a doctor passed me. Then he stopped, turned around, and called me by my name and reassured me that he would take good care of me because he was one of the surgeons who did my surgery. What were the odds of me seeing him in Houma? As you could see, God told me to head back home because he had a doctor waiting to care for me. I began to cry as he said that because it was then I really realized how much God loved and cared for me and the importance of being obedient to his leading.

I was having a tough time in the ER that night, and he stood there all night with me until I was able to rest. I remembered telling him I wanted to give him a gift, but he refused and said the best gift I could give him was to get better. I got discharged the next day, and after being home for three days, I got attacked again in my body.

Maybe it's from the stress, but the city was pitch-black at night, and martial law was in full effect. Dealing with pain and sickness and also going through a catastrophic hurricane could be severely emotional on a person, and as I lay there in my bed in a lot of pain, it was different this time. I hadn't been able to walk down the stairs. I had just been in my bed, not getting any rest because my husband will come every thirty minutes to check on me to make sure I was breathing. Things started to look very bleak from there, and at this point, all I could do was just listen to the word being preached via television, and let me say it's very important to support them.

"So let's not get tired of doing what is good. At just the right time we will reap a harvest of blessing if we don't give up. Therefore, whenever we have the opportunity, we should do good to everyone—especially to those in the family of faith" (Gal 6:9–10 NLT).

By this time, many days had passed, and I was just lying there in pain because there were no close hospitals, and I was not up for the fifty-mile ride. I started to struggle to breathe, and suddenly, I took a really big, deep breath, and then I felt myself starting to ascend upward toward the ceiling. It felt like I was being peeled, like you peel the sticker off a paper, and as I was going through the roof of the house, I began to think, *This is what it feels like to die.* However, I was experiencing so much heavenly peace as I went through the clouds. I began to see the stars, and then immediately, I felt myself being pulled back with a great force! As I came back into my body, I took another deep breath, and my eyes opened. I saw Remus, and I asked him, "Why are you praying?"

He said, "Because you were not breathing, and the closest ambulance was fifty miles away, so I had to do something. I went and got in the devil's face, and then I got in God's face and reminded him of all the promises that is in his word, and then I came back upstairs, and you had started breathing again."

Then he asked me in a sweet, soft voice, "Sweetie, do you want to live or do you want to die?"

I thought about it and said, "I want to live."

Then he shouted to the top of his voice it almost felt like the room shook and said, "Act like it!"

When he shouted it, it was like being spiritually defibrillated, and I jumped up to my feet on my own without any help. All I could say was okay, then he said the most beautiful words to me, "Well, can you fix me something to eat then?"

I had never been so happy to fix a meal in all my life, and I had been up ever since, but it didn't end there because I still had the tube in my back. My next appointment was on his birthday, January 12, 2006, and I remembered him telling me, "Sweetie, you'll have to hurt one more time before you heal, and I'm believing for them to take that tube out of your back because that is the gift that I asked God to give me this year."

A week later, I went to my doctor's appointment in Houma, and he went over my chart and did some other test on me while I waited. He came back and said, "Mrs.

Powell, I have good news for you. We're going to remove that tube out of your back today."

Once he removed the tube out of my back, I kept it as a reminder of how faithful God is.

The next two doctor visits showed no pulmonary sarcoidosis and no problems with my kidney. In fact, my urologist said my one kidney was working like two. I was truly thankful to God that I didn't need dialysis or be put on the list for a transplant after suffering through such a traumatic ordeal with my kidneys.

As you have read my story, it is my prayer that you understand where you are on your road to now. "O taste and see that the Lord [is] good: blessed [is] the man [that] trusteth in him" (Ps 34:8 KJV).

CHAPTER 8

Salvation Road
Repentance Path

After reading this book, you may not have a relationship with Jesus Christ and may want one or you may have drifted away like I did, and that's okay. His arms are stretched wide open to receive you back, and let me tell you, he's absolutely *wonderiffic* in every way. If you will allow him to, Jesus is so eager to get you on the path that was created for you before you were born. Just say this simple prayer and mean it with all of your heart and with everything that is within you.

"Heavenly Father, I ask you to forgive me of my sins, and I confess before you this day that I want Jesus Christ, your Son, who you sent into the world, to be my Lord and Savior, and I boldly state that the devil and everything that embodies him is evicted out of this temple, and I now turn it over completely to you. Thank you, Jesus, for coming into my heart and leading me on the right road now, and as I follow you, I may not understand everything, but I am willing to trust you with my entire life in every area because I now know your plans for me are good and not evil. Thank you, Father, for hearing this prayer, and I can now say in the name of Jesus, my Lord and Savior. Amen"

"This means that anyone who belongs to Christ has become a new person. The old life is gone; a new life has begun!" (2 Cor 5:17 NLT)

CHAPTER 9

The Protection Road

Remus

When my wife asked me to close out her book with this chapter, I must admit that I was a little nervous but honored. Anyone who knows me knows that I'm not a big talker, so for her to ask me this, I knew it had to be from the Lord speaking through her.

When we first met, she began to share some of her life experiences with me. It saddened me as I realized she was another victim of sexual abuse added to the other women I have known and dated. Then I hugged her tightly as I felt so much compassion for her and anger at the perpetrator who committed such a despicable thing to her. Then I proceeded to tell her she didn't have to worry about anyone hurting her ever again as long as I'm around. Funny thing was, what I felt with her was different from the others, and that's when I came to conclude that she was going to be my wife.

Kesha possessed all the characteristics or traits that I was looking (praying, actually) for not just in a wife but also in a friend. As time passed, we got closer, and she shared a little bit more, and my love for her and the kids became stronger. Everything she and I did was kid-friendly as I enjoyed all their company, not just hers. Let me be honest that when she told me it was a family member that sexually abused her and not a distant relative, like a cousin or something, which is bad no matter who does it, a lot of thoughts went through my mind. I was raised to always protect, respect, and take care of those closest to you. Nowadays, it seems like those important values are a thing of the past. Strangely after hearing all the horror stories from the women I've known, I decided that I didn't want any biological children because I knew that if something like that was to happen to them, well, I'm not going to say what I would do. So when God blessed me with my beautiful wife and family, I immediately took ownership of protecting and caring for them.

Our heavenly Father has anointed us men as protectors on this earth. That's why we have law enforcement and military. Our heavenly Father has given us authority over our situations.

"But the Lord, is faithful, he will establish you and guard you against the evil one" (2 Thes 3:3).

Those that are the closest to us are the ones that could harm us the most. We have to be careful who we allow our children around, especially friends and relatives who we notice have certain behaviors from them.

"You'll know them by the obvious fruit of their lives and ministries" (Mt 7:20 TPT).

"Wherefore by their fruits ye shall know them" (Mt 7:20 KJV).

As parents, we need to ask God for wisdom to be a better judge of character. We must pay very close attention to the people around us, their daily behavior and language and habits. Everyone around us gives us warning signs with their behavior and habits. We also have to pay very close attention to our children and listen to them. Our children's behavior will let us know if something is wrong. After a traumatic experience, it can cause our children to become very rebellious because they think no one cares about them and they don't feel safe. As fathers, we always want our children to feel very safe and to be able to come to us with anything they need or want. Also, children should be able to trust their fathers.

My message to all mothers is to never value a relationship over the safety and protection of your children. I have heard countless stories of how children went to their parents about their traumatic experiences and the parents did not believe them, which caused their children to become rebellious. Parents, never be too busy or preoccupied to watch over your children because God has placed them in your custody until they mature into adulthood. Moms, please take the time to ask your children about how their day went and make sure to watch their body language as they do. Usually body language is the biggest giveaway for a person who has just been through trauma, be it mental, sexual, or physical.

Allow me this opportunity to say "*please* be *watch-ful*" because Satan is a vicious devourer of families.

Let us not be so preoccupied with ourselves and not see or bypass what is happening in our lives, families, or communities. Believe it or not, what affects our lives and families definitely affects our communities because that's where we live and are a part of, which influences who our children become and how their lives can change for better or worse.

"Be well balanced and always alert, because your enemy, the devil, roams around incessantly, like a roaring lion looking for its prey to devour. Take a decisive stand against him and resist his every attack with strong, vigorous faith" (1 Pt 5:8–9 TPT).

"Be self-controlled and alert. Your enemy the devil prowls around like a roaring lion looking for someone to devour" (1 Pt 5:8 NIV).

"Be sober, be vigilant; because your adversary the devil, as a roaring lion, walketh about, seeking whom he may devour" (1 Pt 5:8 KJV).

Heavenly Father, I ask that you forgive us for neglecting to protect those whom you've placed in our lives. I ask that you give us the discernment to recognize when an act of abuse of any kind is starting to form and give us the courage to take a bold stand plus the necessary action to keep our loved ones safe. In Jesus's name. Amen.

I want to personally thank you for taking the time to read this book, and may it bring healing to you or someone you know plus help to steer your steps on your road to now!

CHAPTER 10

Discovery Road
Identity Prayer

Kesha

Heavenly Father, I come to you and ask that you forgive me for believing the lies of Satan about who I really am. Please blot out the transgression of my iniquities against you from my bloodline. I take this time to receive my true identity of who I am in Christ Jesus and his never-ending love for me. Help me to understand your purpose, plan, and destiny that you have already put in place for me when you created me in my mother's room. You knew exactly who I would be and become because you make no mistakes. I denounce every demon that I allow to control me, my thoughts, and my actions. I now align myself and choose the lordship of Jesus Christ, and I confess my need for him to live in and through me to become all you have created me to be. My new identity is now safe and secure under your protective custody in Christ Jesus. Amen.

ABOUT THE AUTHOR

Kesha Powell is a wife, mother, and entrepreneur. She was born and raised in New Orleans, Louisiana. Despite undergoing numerous surgeries and being miraculously healed from kidney cancer, she remains steadfast as a walking testimony of God's love, mercy, grace, and faithfulness. Kesha is full of personality and enjoys people who she believes is the greatest creation that God made. Her greatest joy comes in spending quiet time with God and hanging out with her husband, Remus, plus serving alongside with him as ushers at their church of seventeen years. Kesha retired from being a certified MUA to create a skin-care formula—which God gave her in a dream after praying about a solution to help her remove the scars that she had from those surgeries—into a company. Her products can be found at amazon.com and walmart.com.